SPECTRUM
READING

Kindergarten

CREDITS
Editor: Jennifer B. Stith
Cover Design: J.J. Giddings, Nick Pearson, Lynne Schwaner
Interior Design: Lynne Schwaner
Illustrations: Max Porter, Josh Janes, Julie Kinlaw

Spectrum®
An imprint of Carson Dellosa Education
PO Box 35665
Greensboro, NC 27425 USA

Printed in the USA • All rights reserved.
ISBN 978-1-4838-7472-2
01-1122512735

Table of Contents Kindergarten

Introduction 4

Glossary of Terms 6

Chapter 1: Pre-Reading Skills 8

    Same and Different 10

    Classifying 14

    Sequencing 18

Chapter 2: Letters and Sounds 20

    Uppercase Letters 22

    Lowercase Letters 23

    Aa, Bb 24

    Short a 27

    Cc, Dd 28

    A, B, C, and D 31

    Ee, Ff 32

    Short e 35

    Gg, Hh 36

    E, F, G, and H 39

    Ii, Jj 40

    Short i 43

    Kk, Ll 44

    I, J, K, and L 47

    Mm, Nn 48

    Oo, Pp 51

Short o 54

M, N, O, and P 55

Qq, Rr 56

Ss, Tt 59

Q, R, S, and T 62

Uu, Vv 63

Short u 66

Ww, Xx 67

Yy, Zz 70

U, V, W, and Y 73

Matching Letters 74

Matching Letters and Sounds 75

Chapter 3: Rhyming 76

    Rhyming Pictures 78

    Find the Rhyme 80

    Rhyming Match 82

    Rhyming Words 84

Chapter 4: High-Frequency Words 86

    the, can, play, here, jump 88

    run, look, up, down, go 89

    and, to, me, big, little 90

    a, come, find, my, see 91

    we, for, said, you, funny 92

Table of Contents Kindergarten

one, two, three, red, blue, yellow 93

it, is, in, I, where 94

help, make, away, not, ... 95

Chapter 5: Fiction 96

Meet Max 98

Max Plays 100

Look, Max! 102

Max Jumps 104

Max Meets Max 106

Max Meets a Man 108

Max Digs a Hole 110

Max Dreams 112

Max Sees Snow 114

Tired Max 116

Max Looks 118

Max Sees a Cat 120

Max Makes a Splash! 122

Max Horses Around 124

The Big Race 126

The Birthday Dog 128

Hungry Max 130

Max and the Cat Play Catch 132

Max Is Sad 134

Max Goes to a Costume Party 136

Chapter 6: Nonfiction 138

Super Teeth 140

Desert Tracks 142

It All Makes Sense 144

Apples 146

Seals 148

The First Cars 150

Birds 152

10 Reasons to Be a Farmer 154

Know Your Snow! 156

Picture Writing 158

Come, Little Leaves 160

Fish 162

Bats 164

Answer Key 166

Spectrum Introduction

For more than 20 years, Spectrum® workbooks have been the solution for helping students meet and exceed learning goals. Each title in the Spectrum workbook series offers grade-appropriate instruction and reinforcement in an effective sequence for learning success.

Spectrum partners with you in supporting your student's educational journey every step of the way! This book will help them navigate kindergarten reading and will give you the support you need to make sure your student learns everything they need to know. Inside you will find:

Chapter Introductions

These introductions provide useful information about the chapter, which may include:

Before-Reading Activities
These activities help students access background knowledge and set the stage for reading each section topic.

Helpful Definitions/Helpful Word List
These words, arranged in order of appearance in the chapter, help support your student's understanding of the skill or reading selection.

Background Information
This introductory text provides you with background information about specific skills taught in the chapter.

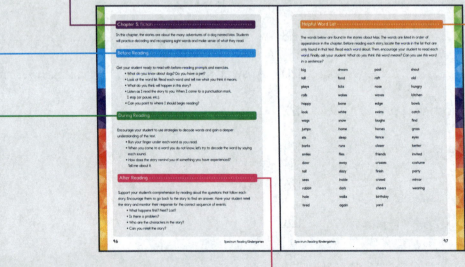

During-Reading Activities
These close-reading strategies help your student read for meaning and understanding.

After-Reading Activities
These activities give your student an opportunity to express what they have learned from the selection.

Reading Selections

These fiction and nonfiction reading selections will cover multiple genres, including fictional stories, informational text, and more. The selections are followed by a series of questions designed to gauge student comprehension.

Selection Prompts

These sentences introduce each reading selection and give your student a quick idea of what they will be reading about in the selection.

Enrichment

These questions appear throughout the book. They allow your student to dig deeper on the story or topic presented. The two types of problems will ask your student to think critically  and explain reasoning.

Engaging Online Practice

Bring learning to life with fun, interactive activities on IXL! Look for the Skill ID and type the 3-digit code into the search bar on IXL.com or the IXL mobile app. Ten questions per day are free!

IXL.com skill ID
2V4

Glossary of Terms

alphabet: the 26 symbols (letters) of the English language

attributes: characteristics of an object, shape, etc.

author: the person or people who write the text

blend: moving from one sound to the next

capital: a letter with the form A. B C, D, E, rather than a, b, c, d, e, and so on

category: a group of people or things that has certain characteristics in common

character: one of the people in a story, book, play, movie, or TV program

compare: to judge one thing in relation to another in order to see the similarities and differences

comprehension: understanding, or the power to understand

consonant: a speech sound or letter that is not a vowel; Examples: *b, k, m* and *r*

contrast: to point out the differences between things

definition: an explanation of the meaning of a word or phrase

detail: items of specific information; small part of a whole item

event: something that happens, especially something that is planned, interesting, or important

fiction: stories about characters and events that are not real

final: last and usually most important

grapheme: a unit of a writing system; letter or letter combinations that represent a phoneme

high-frequency word: a word that appears many times in the English language; Examples: *the, and, is*

illustration: a picture in a book, magazine, or other publication

illustrator: one who creates the pictures for a publication

information: facts and knowledge you get from exploring something, or that you learn by listening

initial: first

language: the use of words to communicate thoughts and feelings

long vowel: a speech sound made with free flow of air through the mouth. Long vowels take a longer time to say and also name the letter. Vowels are represented by the letters *a, e, i, o, u* and sometimes *y*, or combinations of these letters. Example: the *a* sound in *gate*.

lowercase: a letter that is not capital; Examples: *a, b, c, d*

main idea: most important idea

medial: middle

nonfiction: writing about real things, facts, people, and events

phoneme: the sound a letter or letters represent

phrase: more than one word

punctuation: written marks or signs to clarify the meaning of and to separate parts of text

retell: tell the story again in one's own words

rhyme/rhyming: ending sounds correspond, or match

sequence: the order of events or steps

setting: the time and place where a story takes place

short vowel: a speech sound made with free flow of air through the mouth. Short vowels take a shorter time to say. Vowels are represented by the letters *a, e, i, o, u* and sometimes *y*, or combinations of these letters. Example: the *a* sound in *cat*.

syllable: part of a word that includes one vowel sound

uppercase: a letter that is capital in form; Examples: *A, B, C, D*

vowel: a speech sound made with free flow of air through the mouth. These sounds are represented by the letters *a, e, i, o, u* and sometimes *y*, or combinations of these letters

Chapter 1: Pre-Reading Skills

Pre-reading skills are those skills acquired from birth to the time a child learns to read. Print awareness, visual discrimination skills, sorting and classifying, matching, and sequencing are just some of the many skills children practice in their early years of life. As children approach school-age, some of these skills are used to develop print awareness, letter knowledge, narrative skills, and comprehension. Exposing children to books from birth is essential for acquiring language skills. Using alphabet games and puzzles helps strengthen knowledge of sounds and symbols. And, making reading fun and routine helps establish a lifelong desire to read.

A child's developing brain receives input from the eyes and detects differences by using working memory and stored memory. To read, the brain clumps symbols (letters) together to form words. Reading fluency requires being able to tell the difference between letters (especially similar letters such as *b* and *d*), figuring out where a word begins and ends, recognizing familiar words, and decoding.

Below are some definitions and examples to help illustrate the pre-reading skills practiced in this chapter.

Helpful Definitions

Visual discrimination: the ability to notice and name similarities and differences between objects, symbols, figures, etc. based on attributes such as size, color, pattern, texture, orientation, or shape

Matching: determining that two objects are the same

Classifying: being able to assess the items in a group and understand which items belong together because of a certain function or similarity they have

For example, in the group of objects below there are three animals and one tree. A young child should look at the objects and see that the tree is not like the other objects. They should also be able to explain why by using the attributes of the objects to describe their reasoning.

Sequencing: understanding the order of events through pictures or after listening to a story

Chapter 1: Pre-Reading Skills

Same and Different

Draw an X on the object in each row that is different.

Search for this skill ID on IXL.com for more practice!

IXL.com skill ID
8U4

Chapter 1: Pre-Reading Skills

Same and Different

Draw an X on the object in each row that is different.

Chapter 1: Pre-Reading Skills

Same and Different

Draw an X on the object in each row that is different.

Chapter 1: Pre-Reading Skills

Same and Different

Draw an X on the object in each row that is different.

Chapter 1: Pre-Reading Skills

Classifying

Circle the objects in each box that go together.

Search for this skill ID on IXL.com for more practice!

IXL.com skill ID
CME

Chapter 1: Pre-Reading Skills

Classifying

Circle the objects in each box that go together.

Chapter 1: Pre-Reading Skills

Classifying

Draw a line between the objects that go together. The first one has been done for you.

Name _____

Chapter 1: Pre-Reading Skills

Classifying

Circle the objects in each row that go together.

Draw one more object that belongs in this group.

Chapter 1: Pre-Reading Skills

Sequencing

Write **1**, **2**, and **3** to show what happens first, next, and last.

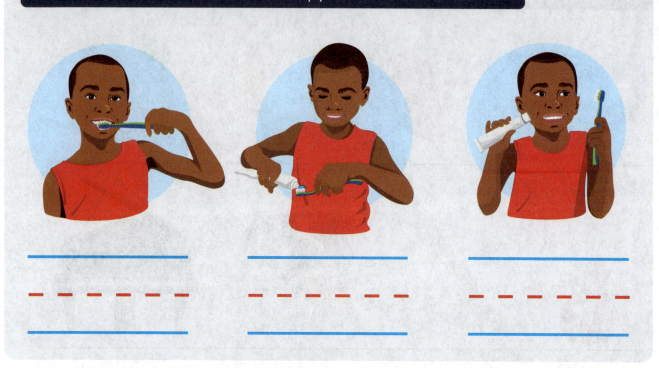

_____
- - - - - - - - -
_____

_____
- - - - - - - - -
_____

Chapter 1: Pre-Reading Skills

Sequencing

Write 1, 2, and 3 to show what happens first, next, and last.

Chapter 2: Letters and Sounds

Because English is an alphabetic language, letter recognition (knowing the names of the letters and the sounds they represent) is a powerful predictor of reading success. Without direct instruction, these abstract symbols are just lines and curves to a child's eyes.

Students must learn the complexities of the alphabet and understand that this system of letters stands for a series of sounds. Students will need to identify differences between similar-looking letters, letter size, letter position, etc.

Adding even more complexity is the fact that they must often memorize four major letter formations of each letter: uppercase manuscript, lowercase manuscript, uppercase cursive, and lowercase cursive.

With time and training, students should name and quickly recognize letters, freeing up "brain power" so that they can focus on more complex tasks during the critical learning-to-read stage.

Helpful Definitions

alphabetic principle: the understanding that the system of letters stands for a series of sounds

A and **a** represent the same sounds.

letter recognition: identifying and naming each letter of the alphabet

phonemic awareness: the understanding that words are made up of a series of distinct sounds

The word **bat** has three sounds: /b/ /a/ /t/

The word **bath** has three sounds: /b/ /a/ /th/

The word **bake** has three sounds: /b/ /a/ /k/

decode: translate a written word into spoken sounds; "sounding out"

uppercase letters: capital letters

A	B	C	D	E	F	G
H	I	J	K	L	M	N
O	P	Q	R	S	T	U
V	W	X	Y	Z		

lowercase letters: non-capital letters

a	b	c	d	e	f	g
h	i	j	k	l	m	n
o	p	q	r	s	t	u
v	w	x	y	z		

letter distinctions: similar-looking letters, reversals, orientations, etc.

b and d are mirror images

E and F look similar

n and u are flipped images

IXL.com
skill ID
2V4

Chapter 2: Letters and Sounds

Uppercase Letters

Point to and say the name of each letter and object.

A 🍎	B 🍌	C 🥕
D 🦆	E 🐘	F 🦊
G 🍇	H 👒	I 🧊
J 🚙	K 🔑	L 🍁
M 🐭	N 🪹	O 🐙
P 🐷	Q 🧩	R 🐰
S ☀️	T 🐢	U ☂️
V 🎻	W ⌚	X 🩻
Y 🪀	Z 🦓	

Search for this
skill ID on IXL.com
for more practice!

IXL.com
skill ID
SVC

Chapter 2: Letters and Sounds

Lowercase Letters

Point to and say the name of each letter and object.

a	🍎	b	🍌	c	🥕
d	🦆	e	🐘	f	🦊
g	🍇	h	🎩	i	⛄
j	🚙	k	🔑	l	🍁
m	🐁	n	🪹	o	🐙
p	🐷	q	🧵	r	🐰
s	☀️	t	🐢	u	☂️
v	🎻	w	⌚	x	🩻
y	🪀	z	🦓		

Chapter 2: Letters and Sounds

Aa, Bb

Circle the matching letters in each row.

Aa    **B**b

A A N C A

a e a o a

B P B C B

b g d b b

Name _____

Chapter 2: Letters and Sounds

Aa, Bb

Trace and write the letters. Circle the objects whose names begin with the same letter.

Chapter 2: Letters and Sounds

Aa, Bb

Trace and write the letters. Write a letter below the objects that begin with that letter.

IXL.com
skill ID
8S3

Chapter 2: Letters and Sounds

Short a

Say the name of each picture. Circle each picture whose name has the sound you hear in the middle of **hat**.

Chapter 2: Letters and Sounds

Cc, Dd

Circle the matching letters in each row.

C c    D d

| C | O | D | C | C |

| c | e | c | c | d |

| D | D | P | D | R |

| d | f | a | d | d |

Name _____

Chapter 2: Letters and Sounds

Cc, Dd

Search for this skill ID on IXL.com for more practice!

IXL.com skill ID **VSH**

Trace and write the letters. Circle the objects whose names begin with the same letter.

Cc

Dd

Name _____

Chapter 2: Letters and Sounds

Cc, Dd

Trace and write the letters. Write a letter below the objects that begin with that letter.

Cc

Dd

Spectrum Reading **Kindergarten**

Name _____

Chapter 2: Letters and Sounds

A, B, C, and D

Say the sound of the letter in each row. Circle each object whose name begins with the same sound.

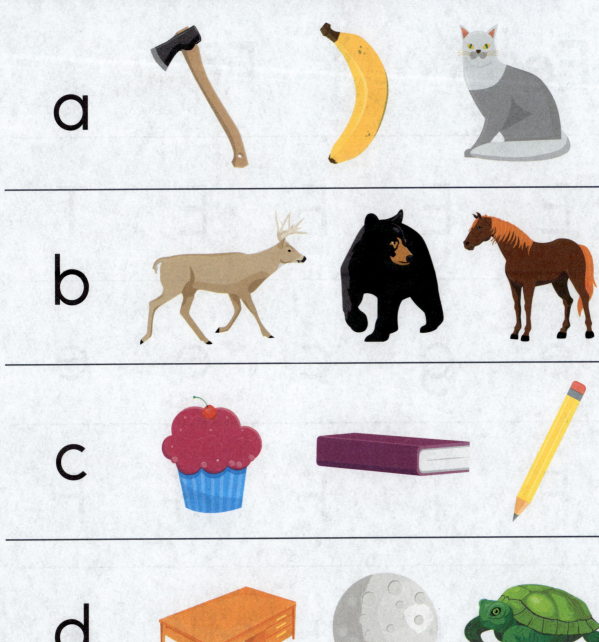

a

b

c

d

Chapter 2: Letters and Sounds

Ee, Ff

> Circle the matching letters in each row.

E e ![elephant]   **F** f ![foot]

| E | E | F | E | T |

| e | g | c | e | e |

| F | T | F | H | F |

| f | f | t | l | f |

Chapter 2: Letters and Sounds

Ee, Ff

Trace and write the letters. Circle the objects whose names begin with the same letter.

Ee, Ff

Trace and write the letters. Write a letter below the objects that begin with that letter.

Ee

Ff

Chapter 2: Letters and Sounds

Short e

> Circle each picture whose name has the sound you hear in the middle of **bed**.

Chapter 2: Letters and Sounds

Gg, Hh

Circle the matching letters in each row.

Gg    Hh

G	C	G	O	G
g	t	j	g	g
H	H	F	H	K
h	k	t	h	h

Name _____

Chapter 2: Letters and Sounds

Gg, Hh

Search for this skill ID on IXL.com for more practice!

IXL.com skill ID **79H**

Trace and write the letters. Circle the objects whose names begin with the same letter.

Chapter 2: Letters and Sounds

Gg, Hh

Trace and write the letters. Write a letter below the objects that begin with that letter.

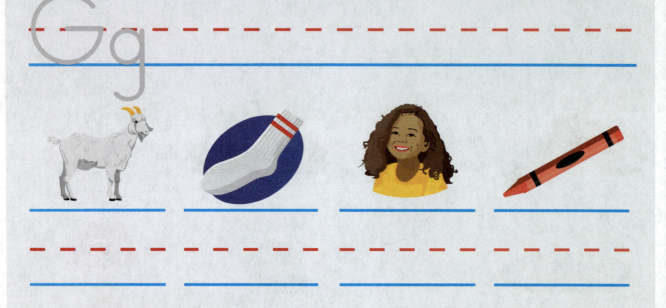

Name _____

Chapter 2: Letters and Sounds

E, F, G, and H

Say the sound of the letter in each row. Circle each object whose name begins with the same sound.

e

f

g

h

Chapter 2: Letters and Sounds

Ii, Jj

Circle the matching letters in each row.

Ii 🏠   Jj ✈️

I	L	N	I	I

i	i	j	l	i

J	D	J	G	J

j	j	y	v	j

Name _____

Chapter 2: Letters and Sounds

Ii, Jj

Trace and write the letters. Circle the objects whose names begin with the same letter.

I i

J j

Name _____

Chapter 2: Letters and Sounds

Ii, Jj

I i

J j

Name _____

Chapter 2: Letters and Sounds

Short i

Circle each object whose name has the sound you hear in the middle of **pig**.

Kk, Ll

Circle the matching letters in each row.

Kk    Ll

K	Y	K	K	U
k	r	k	p	k
L	T	L	H	L
l	l	u	t	l

Name _____

Kk, Ll

> Trace and write the letters. Circle the objects whose names begin with the same letter.

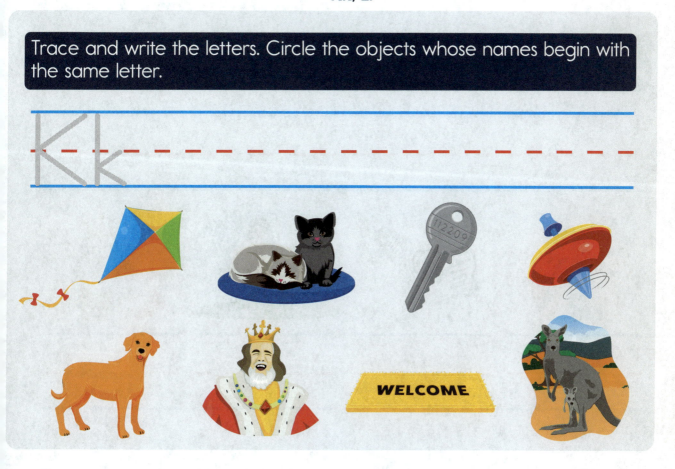

Chapter 2: Letters and Sounds

Kk, Ll

Trace and write the letters. Write a letter below the objects that begin with that letter.

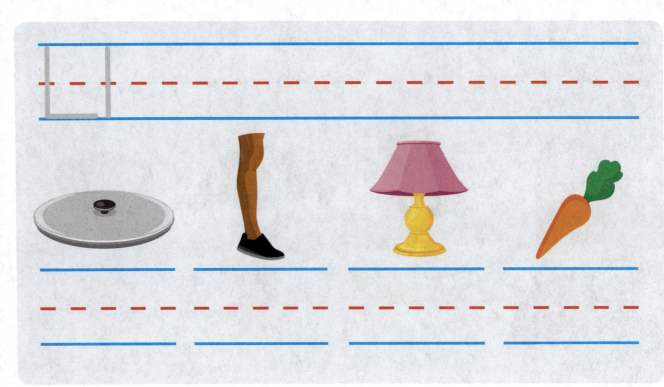

Chapter 2: Letters and Sounds

I, J, K, and L

Say the sound of the letter in each row. Circle each object whose name begins with the same sound.

i

j

k

l

Chapter 2: Letters and Sounds

Mm, Nn

Circle the matching letters in each row.

Mm 🌑   **Nn** 🥅

M	W	M	S	M
m	n	w	m	m
N	M	X	N	N
n	r	n	t	n

Name _____

Chapter 2: Letters and Sounds

IXL.com
skill ID
RVX

Mm, Nn

Trace and write the letters. Circle the objects whose names begin with the same letter.

Mm

Nn

Chapter 2: Letters and Sounds

Mm, Nn

Trace and write the letters. Write a letter below the objects that begin with that letter.

Chapter 2: Letters and Sounds

Oo, Pp

Circle the matching letters in each row.

Oo    Pp

| O | Q | O | U | O |

| o | c | g | o | o |

| P | P | P | F | B |

| p | q | p | r | p |

Chapter 2: Letters and Sounds

Oo, Pp

Trace and write the letters. Circle the objects whose names begin with the same letter.

Name _____

Chapter 2: Letters and Sounds

Oo, Pp

Trace and write the letters. Write a letter below the objects that begin with that letter.

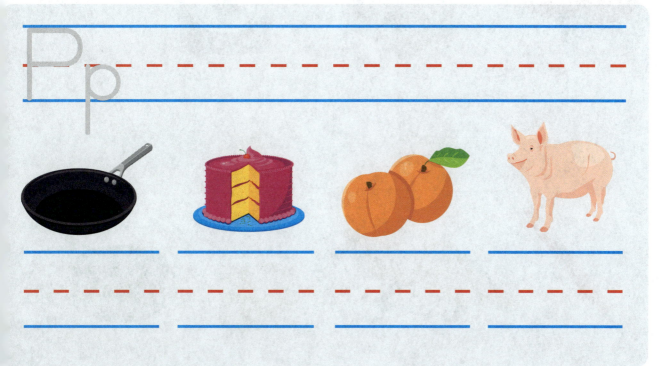

Chapter 2: Letters and Sounds

Short o

Circle each picture whose name has the sound you hear in the middle of **hop.**

Name _____

Search for this skill ID on IXL.com for more practice!

IXL.com skill ID QDV

M, N, O, and P

Say the sound of the letter in each row. Circle each object whose name begins with the same sound.

m

n

o

p

Chapter 2: Letters and Sounds

Qq, Rr

Circle the matching letters in each row.

Q q   **R r**

| Q | Q | O | C | Q |

| q | g | q | p | q |

| R | R | P | R | F |

| r | y | r | r | w |

Chapter 2: Letters and Sounds

Qq, Rr

Trace and write the letters. Circle the objects whose names begin with the same letter.

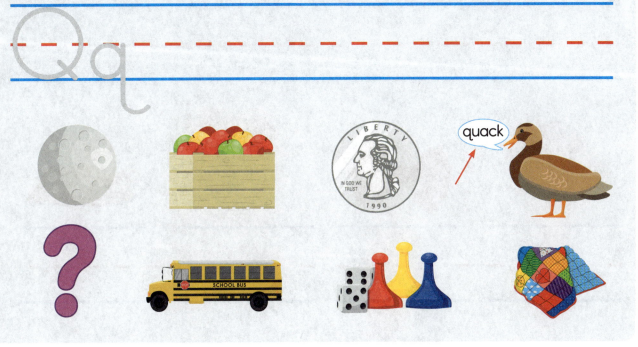

Chapter 2: Letters and Sounds

Qq, Rr

Trace and write the letters. Write a letter below the objects that begin with that letter.

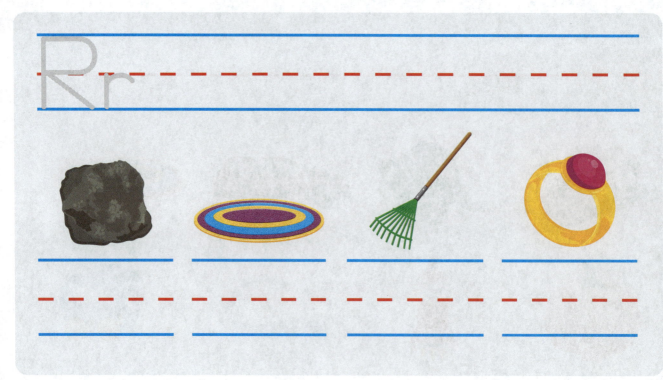

Chapter 2: Letters and Sounds

Ss, Tt

Circle the matching letters in each row.

S	G	S	Y	S

s	t	q	s	s

T	L	T	Y	T

t	I	t	t	y

Name _____

Chapter 2: Letters and Sounds

Ss, Tt

Trace and write the letters. Circle the objects whose names begin with the same letter.

Ss

Tt

Name ______________________________

Chapter 2: Letters and Sounds

Ss, Tt

Trace and write the letters. Write a letter below the objects that begin with that letter.

Ss

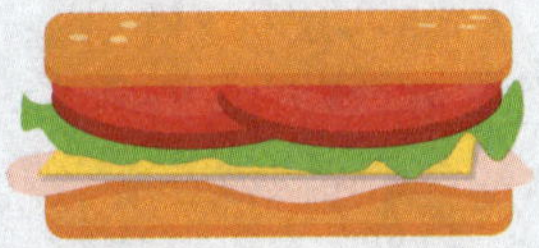 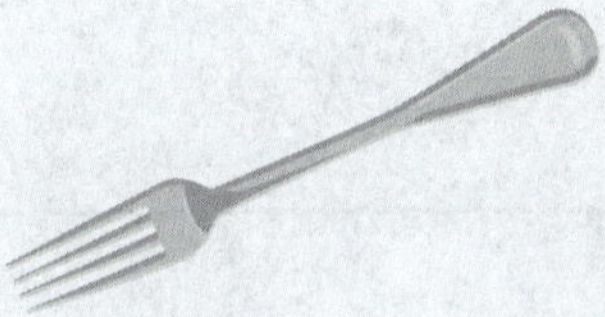 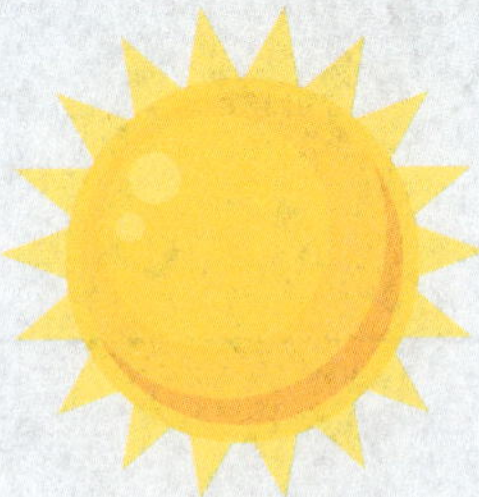 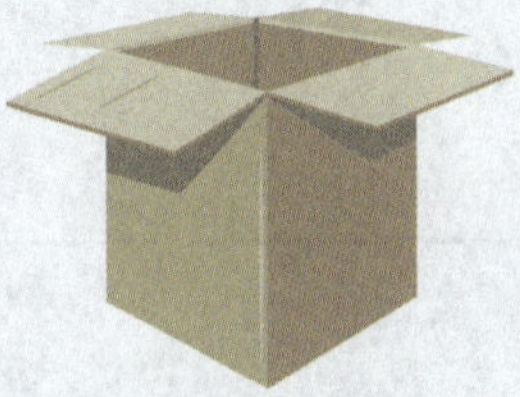

Tt

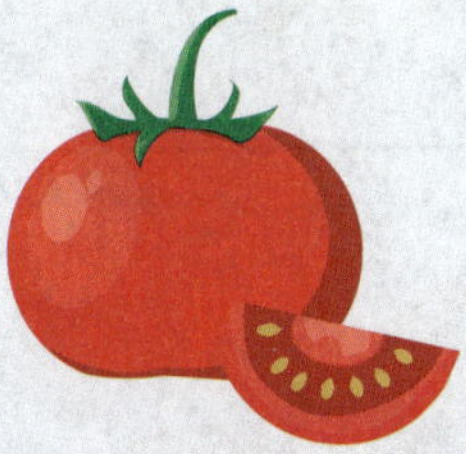 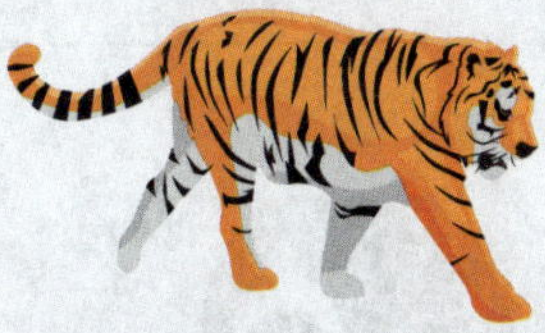 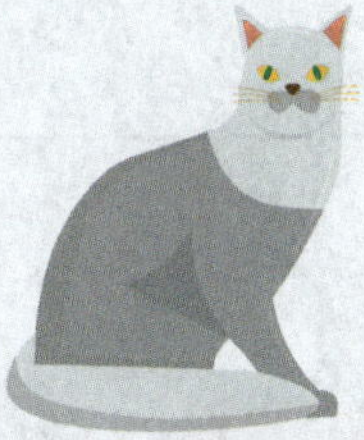 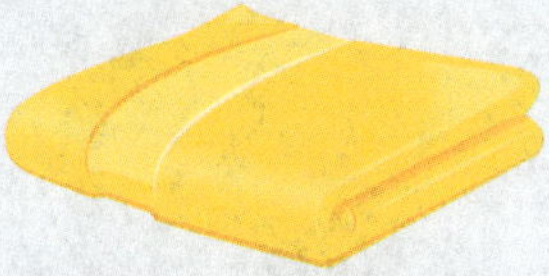

Chapter 2: Letters and Sounds

Q, R, S, and T

Say the sound of the letter in each row. Circle each object whose name begins with the same sound.

q

r

s

t

Search for this
skill ID on IXL.com
for more practice!

IXL.com
skill ID
THX

Chapter 2: Letters and Sounds

Uu, Vv

Circle the matching letters in each row.

U u    V v

U   V   U   W   U

u   u   n   u   v

V   Y   W   V   V

v   v   v   u   w

Chapter 2: Letters and Sounds

Uu, Vv

Trace and write the letters. Circle the objects whose names begin with the same letter.

Uu

Name _____

Chapter 2: Letters and Sounds

Uu, Vv

Trace and write the letters. Write a letter below the objects that begin with that letter.

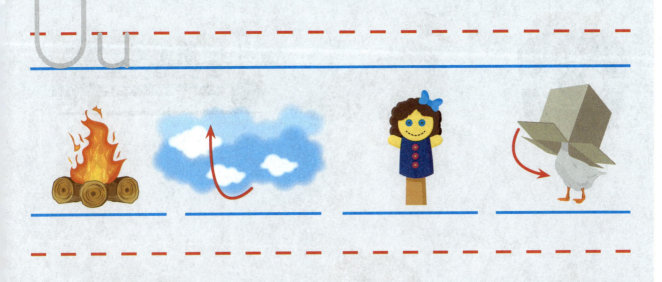

IXL.com
skill ID
G7Q

Chapter 2: Letters and Sounds

Short u

Circle each picture whose name has the sound you hear in the middle of **sun**.

Chapter 2: Letters and Sounds

Ww, Xx

IXL.com
skill ID
NPX

Circle the matching letters in each row.

W w    X x

W	V	W	W	M

w	w	m	w	v

X	Y	A	X	X

x	x	v	x	y

Chapter 2: Letters and Sounds

Ww, Xx

Trace and write the letters. Circle the objects whose names begin with the same letter.

Trace and write the letters. Circle the objects whose names end with the same letter.

Name _____

Chapter 2: Letters and Sounds

Ww, Xx

Trace and write the letters. Write a letter below the objects that begin with that letter.

W w

Trace and write the letters. Circle the objects whose names end with the same letter.

X x

Chapter 2: Letters and Sounds

Yy, Zz

Circle the matching letters in each row.

Y y    Z z

Y	V	N	Y	Y

y	y	f	y	v

Z	A	Z	E	Z

z	s	z	z	n

Name ______________________________

Search for this skill ID on IXL.com for more practice!

IXL.com skill ID **WTM**

Chapter 2: Letters and Sounds

Yy, Zz

Trace and write the letters. Circle the objects whose names begin with the same letter.

Y y

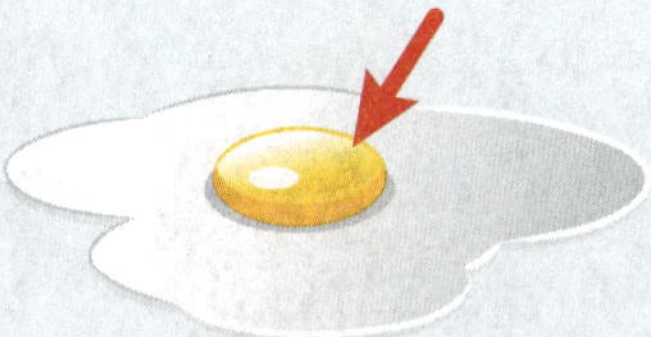
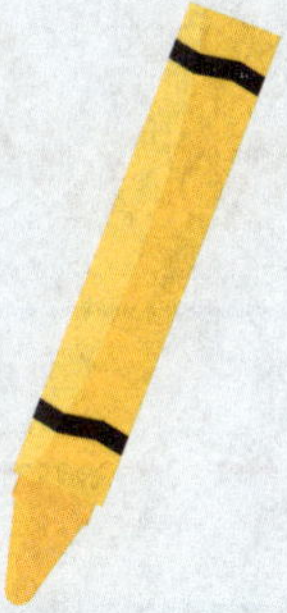
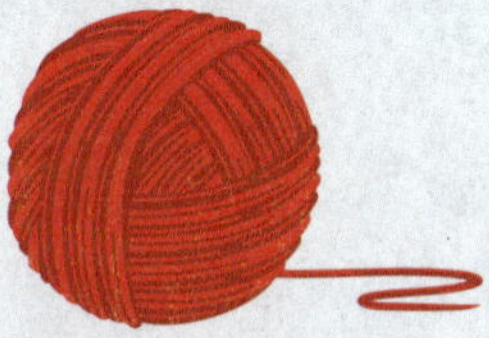
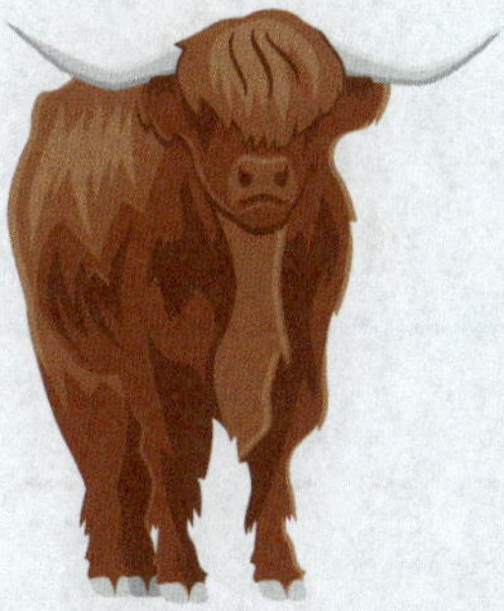
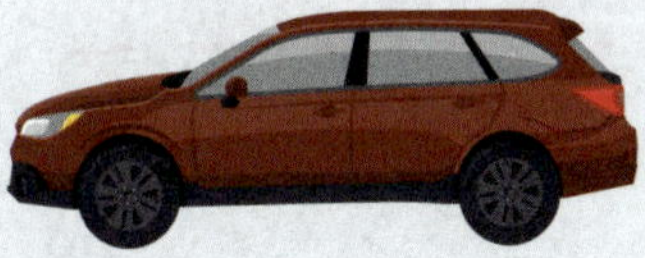
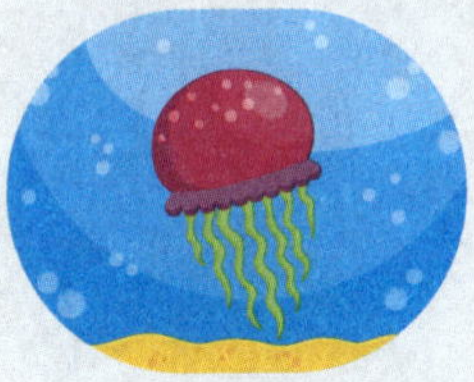

Z z

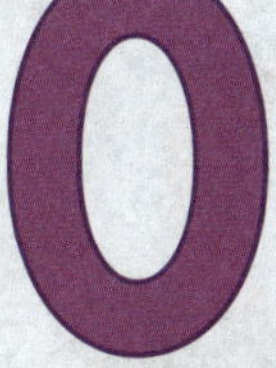
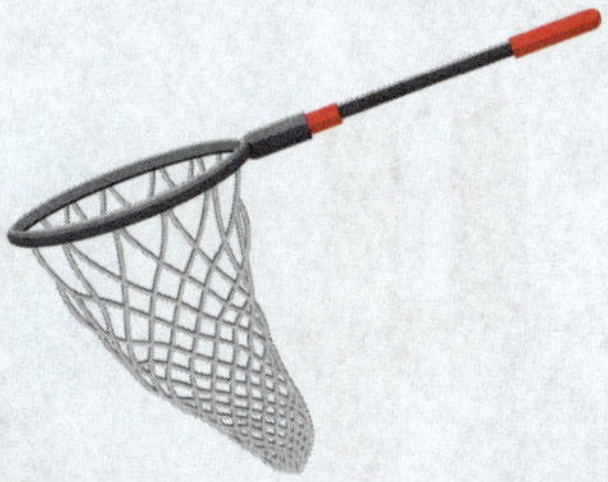
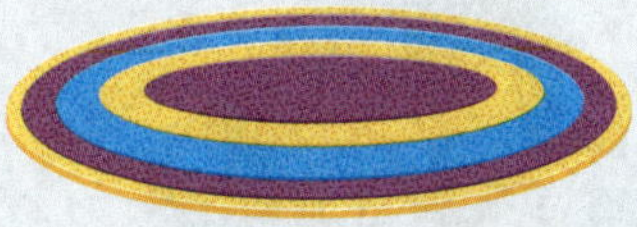
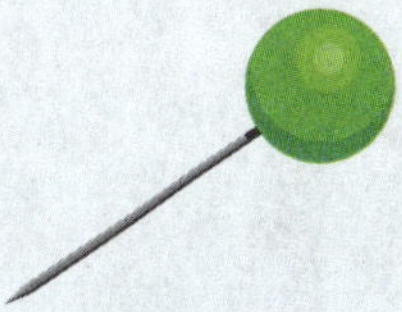
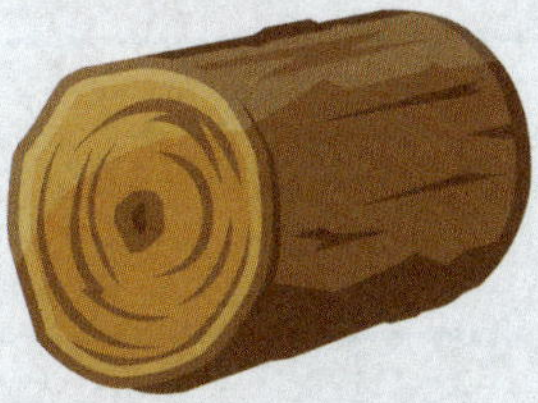
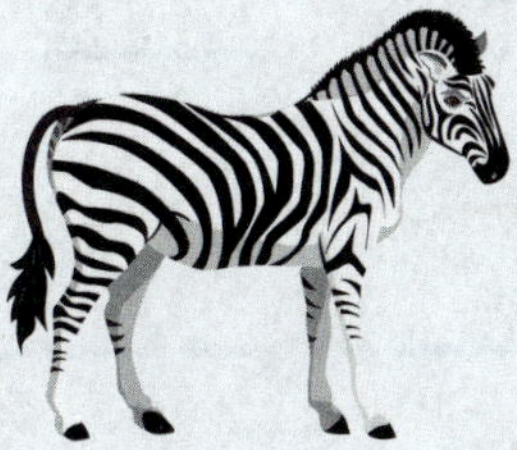
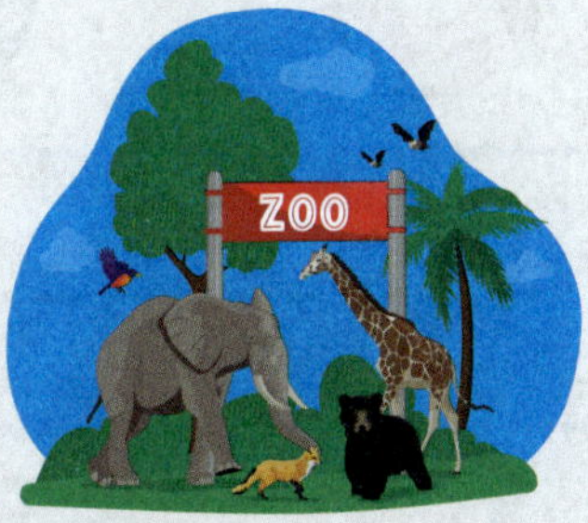

IXL.com
skill ID
8XS

Chapter 2: Letters and Sounds

Yy, Zz

Trace and write the letters. Write a letter below the objects that begin with that letter.

Yy

Zz

Name _____

Chapter 2: Letters and Sounds

U, V, W, and Y

Say the sound of the letter in each row. Circle each object whose name begins with the same sound.

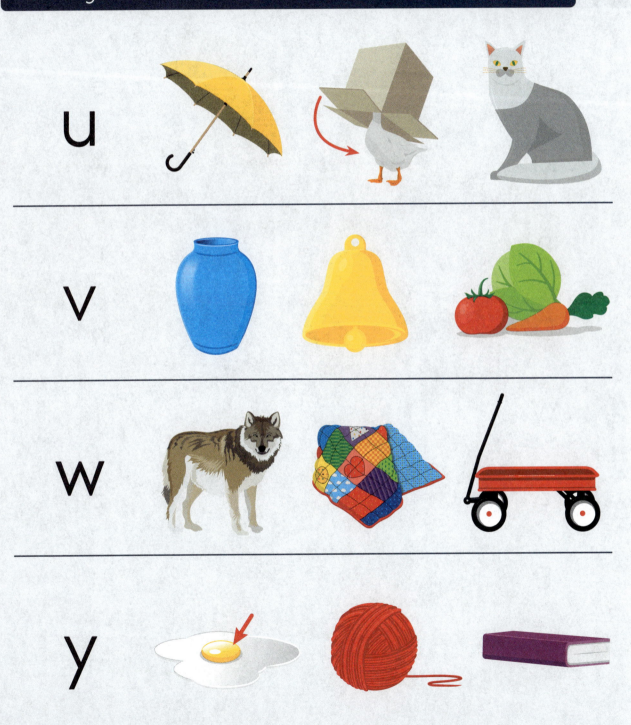

IXL.com
skill ID
6MJ

Chapter 2: Letters and Sounds

Matching Letters

Draw lines to match each uppercase letter to its matching lowercase letter.

H   e

M   w

R   r

D   h

W   j

Z   z

E   d

J   m

Chapter 2: Letters and Sounds

Matching Letters and Sounds

Draw lines to match each letter to the object whose name begins with that letter.

b

p

r

m

f

w

s

h

Chapter 3: Rhyming

Students will begin to recognize phonemes and graphemes of words that belong to the same rhyming word family. Focus on the sounds of the word endings, or rimes. Students should start with simple consonant-vowel-consonant (CVC) words with short vowel sounds. For example, in *cat* and *hat* it is simpler to hear the *-at* word family than in *flat* and *chat*. Adding blends and digraphs can occur once CVC rhymes are mastered.

Have students differentiate sounds amongst three or four images where one image has a different rime.

Have students match or sort pictures by ending sounds. Once students have mastered rhyming phonemes, you can introduce the word family graphemes, or letters. Students can then begin to connect sounds with letters.

Helpful Definitions

rhyme: words that rhyme have the same ending sounds
For example:

can, ran, tan, pan

onset and rime: The onset is the part of a single-syllable word before the vowel. The rime is the part of a word including the vowel and the letters that follow.
For example:

onset	rime
/d/	/og/
/fr/	/og/

grapheme: a letter or combination of letters that represent a single sound
For example:

s*un* has three graphemes: s, u, n

phoneme: a distinct unit of sound in a language

For example:

ship has three phonemes: /sh/, /i/, /p/

word family: a group of words that share a pattern of letters and sounds

For example:

-at word family

bat	pat
cat	rat
hat	sat

blend: two or more letters that come together to form a sound, but each letter retains its own sound

For example:

r-blends	**l-blends**	**s-blends**
brim	blip	scab
crab	club	skip
dress	flag	snap
frog	glad	spin
grab	plan	stem
prod	slip	swim
trip		

digraph: a combination of two letters representing one sound

For example:

digraph ch	**digraph sh**
chop	ship
rich	dish

Chapter 3: Rhyming

Rhyming Pictures

Circle the objects whose names rhyme.

Chapter 3: Rhyming

Rhyming Pictures

Circle the objects whose names rhyme.

Chapter 3: Rhyming

Find the Rhyme

Circle the objects whose names rhyme with the first object in each row.

Name _____

Search for this skill ID on IXL.com for more practice!

IXL.com skill ID
AKH

Chapter 3: Rhyming

Find the Rhyme

Circle the objects whose names rhyme with the first object in each row.

Chapter 3: Rhyming

Rhyming Match

Draw a line from each object to a word that rhymes with its name.

can

bat

sun

wig

hot

Chapter 3: Rhyming

Rhyming Match

Draw a line from each object to a word that rhymes with its name.

rock

tag

red

mop

fun

Rhyming Words

Write the word that rhymes with the first word in each row.

sun

mop

wig

bat

Rhyming Words

Write the word that rhymes with the first word in each row.

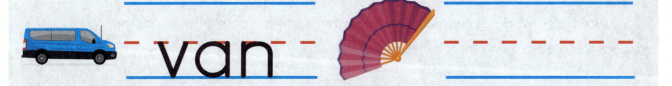

van

dog

cap

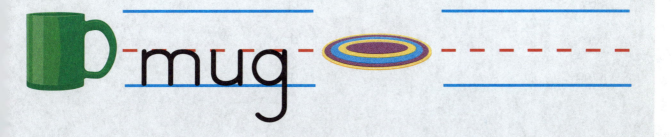

mug

Chapter 4: High-Frequency Words

Recognition of high-frequency words and sight words has an important role in the early phases of learning to read. High-frequency words make up to 50–75% of the words commonly used by children in everyday reading and writing. Getting children to recognize these words quickly is important. Many of these words do not follow phonetics principles, making them difficult to decode.

Many word lists exist, but in general, it is agreed that there is a core list of words that appear more often than others in the English language.

This chapter introduces a few words at a time, practicing with writing the words and reading them in sentences, and completing exercises to reinforce the words. Learning these words offers students a good base for beginning reading as well as building fluency, a key component to reading.

Helpful Definitions and Word List

high-frequency words: words that are most commonly used in reading and writing everyday

sight word: a word that a reader recognizes right away without sounding it out

fluency: the ability to read text accurately, quickly, and with expression

In this chapter, the following words are practiced:

the	run
can	look
play	up
here	down
jump	go

and	one
to	two
me	three
big	red
little	yellow
a	blue
come	it
find	is
my	in
see	I
we	where
for	help
said	make
you	away
funny	not

Name _____

Chapter 4: High-Frequency Words

Read the words in the box. Trace the letters and then read each word.

| the | can | play | here | jump |

the can play

here jump

Read the sentences. Underline the words from the box.

The can jump.

The can play.

The can play here.

The can jump here.

Name _____

Chapter 4: High-Frequency Words

Read the words in the box. Trace the letters and then read each word.

run	look	up	down	go

run   look   up

down   go

Read the sentences. Underline the words from the box.

The  can run.

The  can look.

The ✈ can go up.

The 🚙 can go down the road.

Chapter 4: High-Frequency Words

Read the words in the box. Trace the letters and then read each word.

| and | to | me | big | little |

and to me

big little

Read the sentences. Underline the words from the box.

The big dog can run to me.

The little dog can run to me.

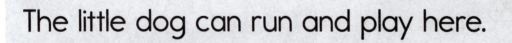

The little dog can run and play here.

The big dog can run and play here.

Chapter 4: High-Frequency Words

Read the words in the box. Trace the letters and then read each word.

a	come	find	my	see

a   come   find

my   see

Read the sentences. Underline the words from the box.

A boy and girl come to see my dog.

The boy and girl find my dog here.

My dog can come up to the boy and girl.

The boy and girl see my dog run and find the food.

Chapter 4: High-Frequency Words

Read the words in the box. Trace the letters and then read each word.

| we | for | said | you | funny |

we for said

you funny

Read the sentences. Underline the words from the box.

Mom said, "You can play ball."

Dad said, "You can play ball here."
The little boy said, "A ball for me!"

"We can play ball," said Dad.

The little boy is funny.

Name _____

Chapter 4: High-Frequency Words

Read the words in the box. Trace the letters and then read each word.

| one | two | three | red | blue | yellow |

one   two   three

red   blue   yellow

Read the sentences. Underline the words from the box.

The little boy said, "I see three boats."

The big boy said, "I see two blue boats."

A little girl said, "I see one red boat."

A big girl said, "I see a yellow boat."

Chapter 4: High-Frequency Words

Read the words in the box. Trace the letters and then read each word.

| it | is | in | I | where |

it   is   in

I   where

Read the sentences. Underline the words from the box.

The girl said, "Where is the car?"

The boy said, "It is in here."

"Where is the ball?" said the girl.

The boy said, "I see the ball in here."

Name _____

Chapter 4: High-Frequency Words

Read the words in the box. Trace the letters and then read each word.

| help | make | away | not |

help make

away not

Read the sentences. Underline the words from the box.

Dad can help the baby.

Dad and Mom can make the baby smile.

They help look for the dog.

The dog did not run away.

Chapter 5: Fiction

In this chapter, the stories are about the many adventures of a dog named Max. Students will practice decoding and recognizing sight words and make sense of what they read.

Before Reading

Get your student ready to read with before-reading prompts and exercises.

- What do you know about dogs? Do you have a pet?
- Look at the word list. Read each word and tell me what you think it means.
- What do you think will happen in this story?
- Listen as I read the story to you. When I come to a punctuation mark, I stop (or pause, etc.).
- Can you point to where I should begin reading?

During Reading

Encourage your student to use strategies to decode words and gain a deeper understanding of the text.

- Run your finger under each word as you read.
- When you come to a word you do not know, let's try to decode the word by saying each sound.
- How does the story remind you of something you have experienced? Tell me about it.

After Reading

Support your student's comprehension by reading aloud the questions that follow each story. Encourage them to go back to the story to find an answer. Have your student retell the story and monitor their response for the correct sequence of events.

- What happens first? Next? Last?
- Is there a problem?
- Who are the characters in the story?
- Can you retell the story?

The words below are found in the stories about Max. The words are listed in order of appearance in the chapter. Before reading each story, locate the words in the list that are only found in that text. Read each word aloud. Then, encourage your student to read each word. Finally, ask your student: *What do you think this word means? Can you use this word in a sentence?*

big	dream	pool	shout
tall	food	raft	old
plays	licks	nose	hungry
rolls	wakes	waves	kitchen
happy	bone	edge	bowls
look	white	swims	catch
wags	snow	laughs	find
jumps	home	horses	grass
sits	sleep	fence	eyes
barks	runs	closer	better
smiles	flies	friends	invited
door	away	crosses	costume
tail	dizzy	finish	party
sees	inside	crowd	mirror
rabbit	dark	cheers	wearing
hole	walks	birthday	
tired	again	yard	

Read the story.

Meet Max

Meet Max.

Max is big.

Max is tall.

Meet Max.

Name _____

Chapter 5: Fiction

Search for this skill ID on IXL.com for more practice!

IXL.com skill ID **RWQ**

Answer the questions.

1. Who is Max?

   _____

2. What do you think he is like?

   _____

   _____

3. How do you think the other animals feel sitting next to Max?

   _____

   _____

4. Circle the sentence that matches the picture.

Max is big.

Max is small.

Chapter 5: Fiction

Read the story.

Max Plays

Max plays.

Max rolls over.

Max rolls over and over.

Max is happy.

Name _____

Chapter 5: Fiction

IXL.com
skill ID
T8Q

Answer the questions.

1. What is Max doing?

   _____

2. How do you think Max feels?

   _____

3. What will Max do next?

   _____

   _____

4. Circle the sentence that matches the picture.

   Max rolls.

   Max hides.

Read the story.

Look, Max!

Look, Max!

Look, Max, look.

Max wags his tail.

Max looks.

Name _____

Chapter 5: Fiction

Answer the questions.

1. What does Max see?

   _____

2. What does Max do?

   _____

3. Why does Max wag his tail?

   _____

4. Circle *yes* or *no*.

Max looks.	yes	no
Max runs away.	yes	no
Max wags his tail.	yes	no
Max eats.	yes	no

Chapter 5: Fiction

Read the story.

Max Jumps

Max looks.

Max plays.

Max jumps.

Jump, Max!

Name _____

Chapter 5: Fiction

Answer the questions.

1. What does Max see?

   _____

2. What is Max doing?

   _____

   _____

3. What happens to the ball?

   _____

   _____

4. Circle the sentence that matches the picture.

   Max loses the ball.

   Max plays with the ball.

Chapter 5: Fiction

Read the story.

Max Meets Max

Max looks.
It looks.

Max sits.
It sits.

Max jumps.
It jumps.

Max wags his tail.
It wags its tail.

Name _____

IXL.com
skill ID
UZL

Answer the questions.

1. What is Max looking into?

    _____

2. What does Max think he sees?

    _____

3. How does Max feel about what he sees?

    _____

4. Circle the sentence that matches the picture.

Max sits.

Max wags his tail.

Read the story.

Max Meets a Man

Max sees a man.
Max sits up.

Max sees the man.
Max barks.

Max jumps.
Max barks again.

Max wags his tail.
The man smiles.

Name _____

Chapter 5: Fiction

Answer the questions.

1. What does Max see?

   _____

2. Why do you think Max barks?

   _____

   _____

3. Why do you think Max wags his tail?

   _____

   _____

4. Circle the word in the story that tells the man is happy to see Max.

Chapter 5: Fiction

> **Read the story.**

Max Digs a Hole

Max sees a rabbit.

The rabbit runs into a hole.
Can the rabbit play?

Max digs a bigger hole.

Max is tired.

Chapter 5: Fiction

Answer the questions.

1. What kind of animal does Max see?

   _____

2. What does Max want the rabbit to do?

   _____

3. What is Max doing now?

   _____

4. Circle the word that completes the sentence.

   The rabbit runs into a _____.

        tree   house   hole

Chapter 5: Fiction

Read the story.

Max Dreams

Max sleeps.
Max is dreaming.

Max dreams about
a bone.
Max smiles.

Max licks his lips.
Max wags his tail.

Max wakes up.
A boy gives Max a
bone.

Name _____

Chapter 5: Fiction

Answer the questions.

1. What do you think Max is dreaming about?

    _____

2. Did Max's dream come true?

    _____

Draw a picture of what you dream about.

Name _____

Read the story.

Max Sees Snow

Max sees white things.

Max feels the snow.

Come back, Max!

Max comes home.
Sleep, Max, sleep.

Chapter 5: Fiction

Answer the questions.

1. What is happening?

   _____

2. What does Max do?

   _____

3. Why is Max running?

   _____

4. Circle the word that completes the sentence.

   The snow is _____ .

   blue   white   green

Chapter 5: Fiction

Read the story.

Tired Max

Max sees a bird.
He wants to play.

Max runs after it.
Max runs and runs.

The bird flies away.

Max stops.
He is tired.

Chapter 5: Fiction

Answer the questions.

1. What does Max see?

   _____

2. How do you think Max feels when he chases the bird?

   _____

3. What happened to Max?

   _____

4. Circle *yes* or *no*.

Max runs after the bird.	yes	no
Max is tired.	yes	no
The bird stands still.	yes	no
Max catches the bird.	yes	no

Chapter 5: Fiction

Read the story.

Max Looks

Max sees a hole.

Max looks inside.
It is dark.

Run, Max, run!

Max goes home.

Name _____

Chapter 5: Fiction

Answer the questions.

1. What does Max do?

   _____

2. Circle the word that completes the sentence.

   It is _____ inside the hole.

   small   dark   light

3. Why does Max run?

   _____

   Draw what you think scared Max.

Name _____

Chapter 5: Fiction

Read the story.

Max Sees a Cat

Max sees a cat.
The cat sits.

Max smiles.
The cat sits.

Max wags his tail.
The cat sits.

Max sits.
The cat smiles
back.

Search for this
skill ID on IXL.com
for more practice!

IXL.com
skill ID
F6S

Chapter 5: Fiction

Answer the questions.

1. What does Max see?

    _____

2. Circle the word that completes the sentence.

    The cat _____.

    purrs   sits   sleeps

3. How does Max get the cat to smile back?

    _____

    _____

4. Circle the sentence that tells what happens next.

    Max wags his tail.

    The cat sits.

    The cat smiles back.

Chapter 5: Fiction

Read the story.

Max Makes a Splash!

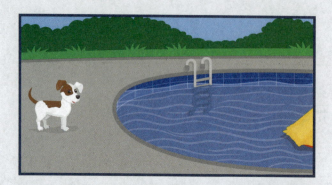

Max sees the pool.
Max walks to the pool.

A girl is lying on a raft.
Max puts his nose in the water.

"Come in, Max!"
The girl waves her hand.

Max jumps into the pool.
The girl laughs.

Chapter 5: Fiction

Answer the questions.

1. Why does Max put his nose in the water?

    _____

2. Why do you think the girl wants Max to come into the pool?

    _____

3. Why does the girl laugh?

    _____

Have you had fun in a pool? Draw a picture of yourself in a pool.

Chapter 5: Fiction

> Read the story.

Max Horses Around

Max sees horses.

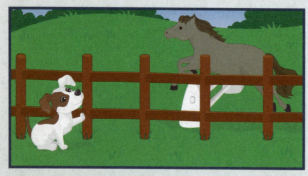

Max watches a horse jump.
Max wants to jump too.

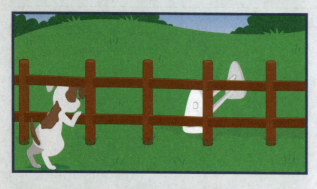

Max tries to jump over the fence.
Max tries, but he falls.

The horses look at Max.
Max looks up at them.

Chapter 5: Fiction

Answer the questions.

1. Circle the word that best completes the sentence.

   Max sees _____.

   horses   cows   goats

2. Why do you think Max wants to jump?

   _____

3. Why do you think the horses stop to look at Max?

   _____

4. What happens to Max?

   _____

Chapter 5: Fiction

Read the story.

The Big Race

Max sits at the line.
Max looks at his
friends.

Get ready, Max.
"Go!" says the boy.
Max runs.

Max is first.
He wins the race.

The crowd cheers.
Max is the winner.

Name _____

Chapter 5: Fiction

Answer the questions.

1. What are Max and his friends going to do?

    _____

2. Who wins the race?

    _____

3. How do you think Max feels?

    _____

 Pretend you are the cat or the bird. What is something you might say to Max?

_____

_____

Chapter 5: Fiction

Read the story.

The Birthday Dog

It is Max's birthday. He is so happy.

Max walks into the yard. He sees his friends.

They all yell, "Happy Birthday, Max! How old are you now?"

Max smiles. He barks five times.

Name _____

Chapter 5: Fiction

Answer the questions.

1. Why is the day special to Max?

   _____

2. Who does Max see in the yard?

   _____

3. Why does Max bark five times?

   _____

 Draw a birthday cake for Max.

Chapter 5: Fiction

Read the story.

Hungry Max

Max is hungry.
Max looks around
for food.

Max looks at the
bowls.
Max eats the cat's
food.

Max looks up.
He looks funny.

The cat comes in.
The cat looks at
Max. The cat smiles.

Name _____

IXL.com
skill ID
DY9

Answer the questions.

1. How does the illustrator show how Max feels?

_____

2. Why do you think Max eats from the cat's bowl?

_____

3. How do you think Max feels right now?

_____

_____

Imagine tasting something you do not like. What would your face look like? Draw a picture.

Chapter 5: Fiction

Read the story.

Max and the Cat Play Catch

Max says hello to the cat. They go outside.

Max and the cat find a ball. They play catch.

Max throws the ball over the cat's head. The cat looks up at the ball.

The ball goes into the pool. Max jumps into the pool. The cat smiles.

Name _____

Chapter 5: Fiction

Answer the questions.

1. What do Max and the cat play?

   _____

2. What do you think will happen next?

   _____

   _____

3. Why do you think the cat is smiling?

   _____

   _____

Read the story.

Max Is Sad

Max is sad.
He lost his bone.

Max walks outside.
He lies down on
the grass.

Max closes his eyes.
The cat comes
outside.

The cat hugs Max.
Max feels better.

Spectrum Reading **Kindergarten**

Name _____

Chapter 5: Fiction

Answer the questions.

1. Why is Max sad?

_____

2. Circle the word that completes the sentence.

Max lies down on the _____.

    grass   bone   ball

3. What does the cat do to make Max feel better?

_____

_____

 Think of a time you lost something. Did you feel the same as Max or different? Share with a friend or family member.

Chapter 5: Fiction

Read the story.

Max Goes to a Costume Party

Max is invited to a costume party.
Max wants to wear a costume.

Max puts on a cat costume.
He looks in the mirror. He laughs.

Max walks to the costume party at a friend's house. The cat opens the door.

The cat is wearing a dog costume.
Max laughs. The cat laughs even harder.

Name _____

Chapter 5: Fiction

Search for this skill ID on IXL.com for more practice!

IXL.com skill ID DTP

Answer the questions.

1. Why does Max laugh when he looks in the mirror?

   _____

2. Where is the costume party?

   _____

3. What is funny about how Max and the cat are dressed?

   _____

Draw a picture of yourself in a funny costume.

Chapter 6: Nonfiction

This chapter includes nonfiction texts in a variety of formats. Some reading selections are presented as infographics. Read aloud the parts of the text and use the images to support comprehension.

Before Reading

Get your student ready to read with before-reading prompts and exercises.

- Let's read the title. What do you know about this topic? What do you want to know?
- Look at the word list. Help your student read each word and talk about its meaning.
- Read the text to your student first to model reading nonfiction texts that have text features, such as captions and sidebars.
- Have your student point to where they should begin reading. (This is not as important with the infographics.)

During Reading

Encourage your student to use strategies to decode words and gain a deeper understanding of the text.

- Run your finger under each word as you read.
- When you come to a word you do not know, let's try to decode the word by saying each sound.
- How does the text remind you of something you have learned? Tell me about it.
- Do you have questions about what you are reading?

After Reading

Support your student's comprehension by reading aloud the questions that follow each text. Encourage them to go back to the text to find an answer. They can answer orally or with words and pictures.

- What does the picture show?
- Can you point to the sentence that tells the answer?
- Can you tell me what you learned in the text?

The words below are found in the reading selections in this chapter. The words are listed in order of appearance. Before reading each nonfiction text, locate the words from the list that appear in that text. Read each word aloud. Then, encourage your student to read each word. Ask, *What do you think this word means? Can you use this word in a sentence?*

strong	strained	harvest
teeth	useful	machine
floss	seal	snow
brush	mammal	freezes
desert	flippers	past
tracks	layer	caves
footprints	temperature	drawings
senses	enough	autumn
sight	cost	fluttering
hearing	bumper	whirling
taste	wings	content
smell	beak	gills
touch	bill	fin
brain	lay	surface
bitter	hatch	bounce
apple	farmer	nectar
grow	community	pollen

What keeps your teeth healthy?

Super Teeth

Your teeth help you chew.

Your teeth help you speak.

Your teeth help you look your best!

  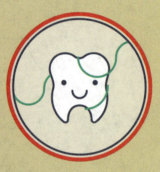

Use just a little bit.   **Take your time.**   **Floss like a boss!**

Eat a lot of these,   **not a lot of these!**

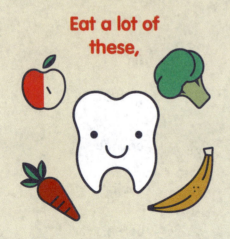 

Chapter 6: Nonfiction

Answer the questions about *Super Teeth*.

1. Teeth are important because they help you

   _____ your food.

2. You should squeeze a lot of toothpaste on your toothbrush.

   True   False

3. You should take your time when you brush your teeth.

   True   False

4. What three things do you need to keep your teeth healthy?

   _____ _____ _____

5. Why do you think the tooth with fruits and vegetables around it looks happy?

   _____

   _____

Chapter 6: Nonfiction

Who made the tracks in the sand?

Desert Tracks
The desert is a hot and dry place.
It does not rain very much. Animal tracks
are easy to see in the dry sand.

Bobcat

Gopher snake

Kit fox

Mule deer

Jackrabbit

There are also many plants in the desert.
They do not need a lot of water to survive.

Chapter 6: Nonfiction

Answer the questions about *Desert Tracks*.

1. It is easy to see animal tracks in the desert because it does not

   _____ much there.

2. How many bobcat footprints do you count?

   _____

3. Which animal left a track that was not a footprint?

   _____

4. There are no plants in the desert.   True   False

Where have you seen an animal track? What animal do you think it belonged to?

_____

_____

Chapter 6: Nonfiction

What are the five senses?

It All Makes Sense

You use your five senses every day
to understand the world around you.

Sight
Your eyes tell your brain what they see.

Smell
Your nose tells your brain what it smells.

Hearing
Your ears tell your brain what they hear.

Touch
Your skin tells your brain what it feels.

Taste
Your tongue tells your brain what it tastes.

BITTER
SALTY
SALTY
SOUR
SOUR
SWEET

Name _____

IXL.com
skill ID
A84

Answer the questions about *It All Makes Sense.*

1. What are your five senses?

   _____   _____

   _____   _____

   _____

2. The bitter taste buds are found at the _____
   of the tongue.

3. Ears tell your brain what they hear.

         True   False

 What is your favorite smell? Why?

   _____

   _____

Chapter 6: Nonfiction

What are apples?

Apples

Apples grow on trees. They are a kind of fruit. They have seeds inside.

People pick apples to eat. Some apples are soft and taste sweet. Others are crisp and taste tart.

Apples can be cooked to make applesauce. Apples can be mashed and strained to make apple juice. Apples can be baked in a pie. Apples are useful for so many things.

Spectrum Reading **Kindergarten**

Chapter 6: Nonfiction

Answer the questions about *Apples*.

1. Where do apples grow?

   _____

   _____

2. What kind of food is an apple?

   _____

   _____

3. How can apples taste?

   _____

   _____

Do you like apples? Why or why not?

_____

_____

Name _____

Chapter 6: Nonfiction

Read all about seals.

Seals

Seals are water mammals that also like land. Some seals stay in the sea for weeks or months at a time. They even sleep in the water. But all seals need land at times. They pick land spots away from people and other animals.

There are 32 different kinds of seals. Their flippers make them very good swimmers and divers. They can stay underwater for as long as 30 minutes.

Seals can live in cold temperatures. They have fur and a thick layer of fat to keep them warm.

Name _____

Chapter 6: Nonfiction

Answer the questions about *Seals*.

1. Where are two places seals live?

   _____ and _____

2. What do seals have that make them good swimmers and divers?

   _____

   _____

3. What keeps seals warm when the air is cold?

   _____

   _____

What does the author say that seals do in water that surprises you? Write the sentence.

   _____

   _____

Chapter 6: Nonfiction

Who built the first cars?

The First Cars

Henry Ford made cars. He built the first cars that were low enough in price for many people to buy them.

Ford's cars were different from the cars that you see today. They could not go as fast. They did not come in as many colors. The gas tank was under the driver's seat. You would have to spend extra money for bumpers and mirrors.

Still, the cars were a great way to get around, just as our cars are today.

Search for this skill ID on IXL.com for more practice!

IXL.com skill ID
RZ8

Chapter 6: Nonfiction

Answer the questions about *The First Cars*.

1. What did Henry Ford do?

   _____

2. Most people could buy these cars. Underline the sentence in the text that tells why.

3. What parts of a car cost extra money?

   _____

   _____

The cars of the past were different from cars of today. Write one difference from the text.

_____

_____

_____

Chapter 6: Nonfiction

What is unique about birds?

Birds

All birds have wings, feathers, and beaks or bills. Most birds fly. But, some birds only walk or run. Penguins and ostriches do not fly.

All birds lay eggs that hatch into baby birds. Most birds lay their eggs in nests. The mother and father birds feed the baby birds until they can find their own food. Many birds eat seeds or insects. Others eat lizards and snakes.

Chapter 6: Nonfiction

Answer the questions about *Birds*.

1. What do all birds have?

   _____

   _____

2. What are two birds that do not fly?

   _____

   _____

3. What do birds eat?

   _____

   _____

Underline the sentence in the text that tells how birds take care of their young.

Chapter 6: Nonfiction

Would you like to be a farmer?

10 Reasons to Be a Farmer

1 You get to feed the world.

6  You can get dirty.

2  You get to work with your community.

7  You get to work with animals.

3  You can be proud of your harvest.

8  You can be around your family all day.

4  You get to work outside.

9 You get to care for the land.

5  You get to ride on farm machines.

10  You will always have a job!

Name _____

Chapter 6: Nonfiction

Answer the questions about *10 Reasons to Be a Farmer*.

1. Why would farmers get dirty?

   _____

2. What do you think *to harvest* means?

   to ride a tractor   to pick the crops you grow

   to feed animals   to save money

3. Farmers get to work with their community.

   True   False

What do you think the best reason to be a farmer is?
Why?

_____

_____

Chapter 6: Nonfiction

What is snow made of?

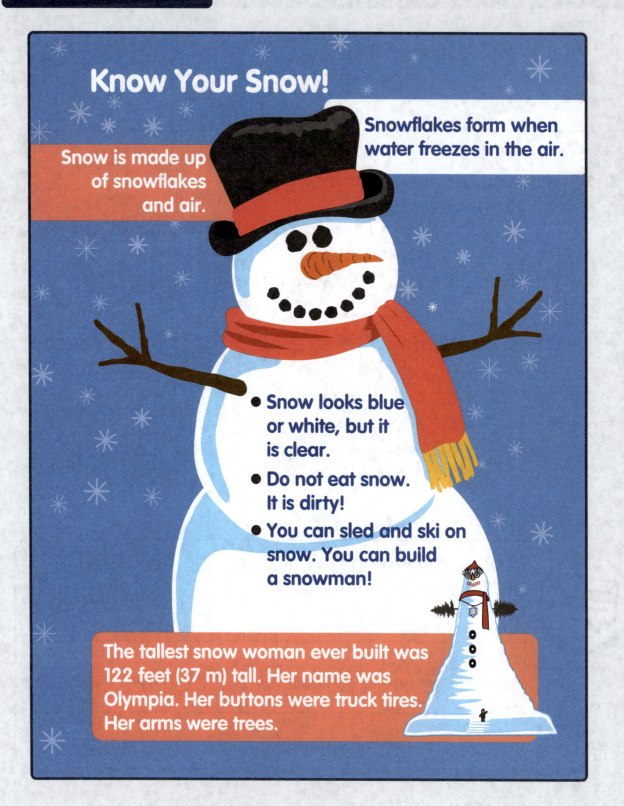

Know Your Snow!

Snow is made up of snowflakes and air.

Snowflakes form when water freezes in the air.

- Snow looks blue or white, but it is clear.
- Do not eat snow. It is dirty!
- You can sled and ski on snow. You can build a snowman!

The tallest snow woman ever built was 122 feet (37 m) tall. Her name was Olympia. Her buttons were truck tires. Her arms were trees.

Name _____

Chapter 6: Nonfiction

Answer the questions about *Know Your Snow!*

1. _____ is made of snowflakes and air.

2. You should eat snow.

      True   False

3. Snowflakes form when water freezes.

      True   False

4. The tallest snow woman ever built was _____ feet tall.

Imagine you build the tallest snow kid. Draw a picture of your snow kid.

Chapter 6: Nonfiction

How did people in the past record their lives?

Picture Writing

A long time ago, people drew pictures to tell stories. These drawings have been found on walls of caves. People used pictures to tell about hunting and growing food. They also drew pictures of their families.

Today, we write stories about our lives. These stories are made up of letters and words instead of pictures.

Name _____

Chapter 6: Nonfiction

Answer the questions about *Picture Writing*.

1. What does the picture show?

    _____

    _____

2. What do the drawings from long ago tell?

    _____

    _____

3. What does the author say we do today to tell about our lives?

    _____

How are the pictures on the cave wall and the words that we read and write the same?

_____

_____

Chapter 6: Nonfiction

Read a poem about autumn leaves.

Come, Little Leaves
by George Cooper

"Come, little leaves," said the wind one day,
"Come over the meadows with me and play;
Put on your dresses of red and gold,
For summer is gone and the days grow cold."

Soon as the leaves heard the wind's loud call,
Down they came fluttering, one and all;
Over the brown fields they danced and flew,
singing the glad little songs they knew.

Dancing and whirling, the little leaves went;
Winter had called them, and they were content;
soon, fast asleep in their earthy beds,
The snow laid a cover over their heads.

Name _____

Chapter 6: Nonfiction

Answer the questions about "Come, Little Leaves."

1. What colors are leaves in autumn?

   _____ and _____

2. What happens to the leaves when the wind comes?

   _____

   _____

3. What do the words *dance* and *sing* make you picture when you read this poem?

   _____

   _____

   _____

4. Leaves are now on the ground. Underline the sentence in the poem that tells what covers them.

Chapter 6: Nonfiction

What features do fish have?

Fish

Fish live in water. A fish uses gills to breathe in the water. Fish cannot breathe without water.

Fish have body parts to help them move in water. A fish uses fins to swim in the water. A fish has a tail so that it can turn in the water. Fins and tails come in all shapes and sizes.

Different fish eat different things. Some fish eat plants. Some fish eat other fish. Some fish eat bugs on the water's surface.

Chapter 6: Nonfiction

Answer the questions about *Fish*.

1. Where does a fish live?

   _____

2. What does a fish use to breathe in the water?

   _____

3. What do fish eat in the water?

   _____

   _____

4. Underline in the text the two body parts that help a fish move. Write the names of the parts.

   _____

   _____

Chapter 6: Nonfiction

Read all about bats.

Bats

Most people do not know how helpful bats are. Bats are one of our best bug catchers. Bats use their mouths and ears to find insects. They make sounds that bounce off of things. This helps them find where the insects are. Bats catch mosquitoes and moths.

Most bats eat just insects. But, some bats eat fruit or nectar from flowers. Bats spread seeds from the fruit. Bats also spread pollen from flowers. Bats help mango, guava, and some nut trees.

Search for this
skill ID on IXL.com
for more practice!

IXL.com
skill ID
JCG

Chapter 6: Nonfiction

Answer the questions about *Bats*.

1. What do bats use to find insects?

   _____

2. What kinds of insects do bats eat?

   _____

3. How do bats help trees?

   _____

   _____

4. Do you think the author likes or dislikes bats? How do you know?

   _____

   _____

   _____

Answer Key

page 10

page 11

page 12

page 13

Answer Key

page 14

page 15

page 16

page 17

Answer Key

page 18

page 19

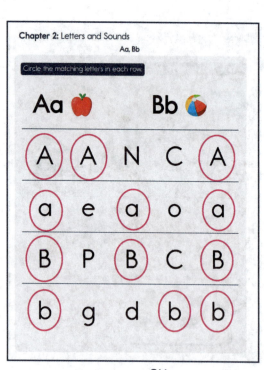

page 24

page 25

Answer Key

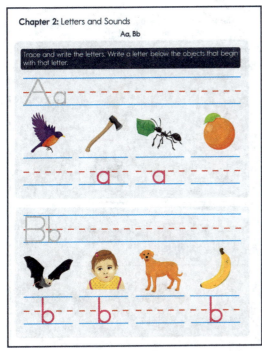

page 26

page 27

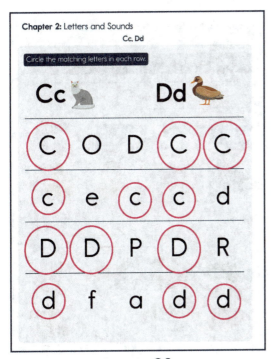

page 28

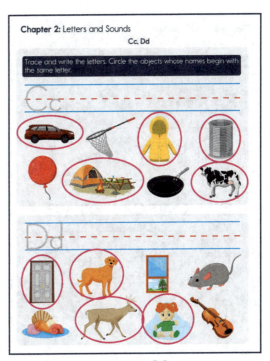

page 29

Answer Key

page 30

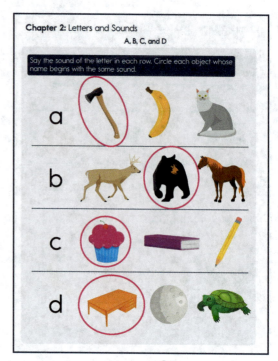

page 31

page 32

page 33

Answer Key

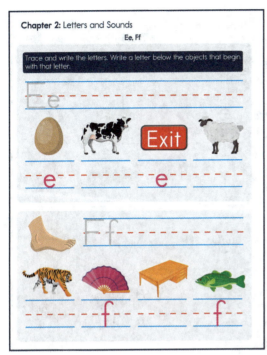

page 34

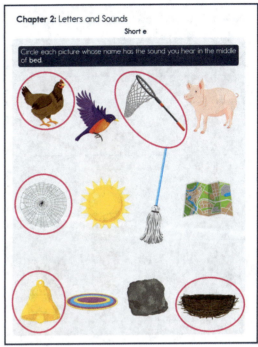

page 35

page 36

page 37

Answer Key

page 38

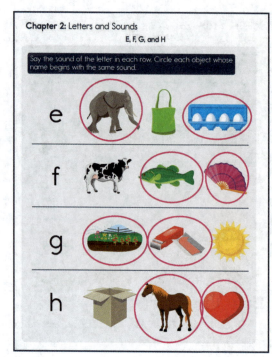

page 39

page 40

page 41

Answer Key

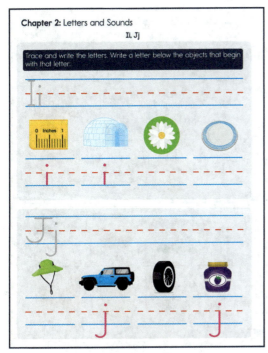

page 42

page 43

page 44

page 45

Answer Key

page 46

page 47

page 48

page 49

Answer Key

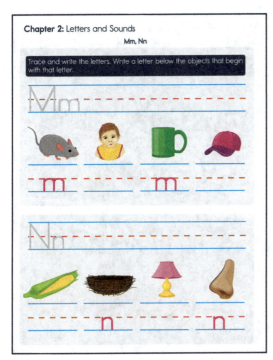

page 50

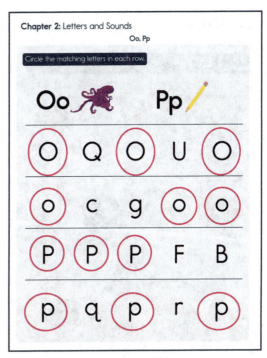

page 51

page 52

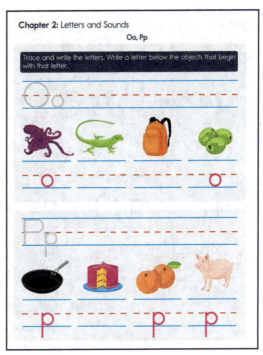

page 53

Answer Key

page 54

page 55

page 56

page 57

Answer Key

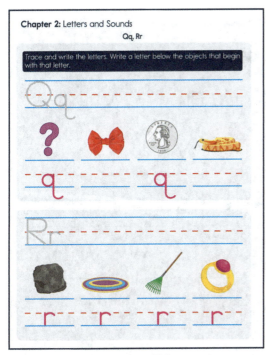

page 58

page 59

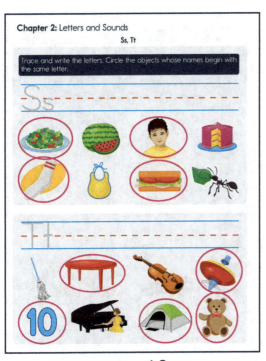

page 60

page 61

Answer Key

page 62

page 63

page 64

page 65

Answer Key

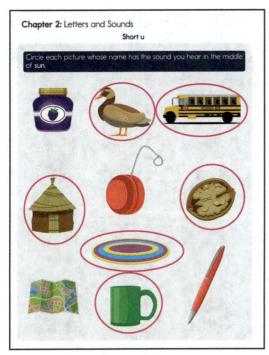

page 66

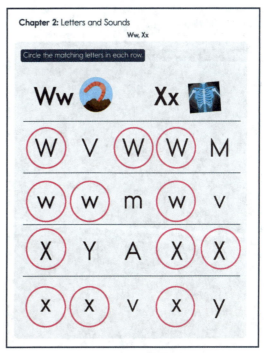

page 67

page 68

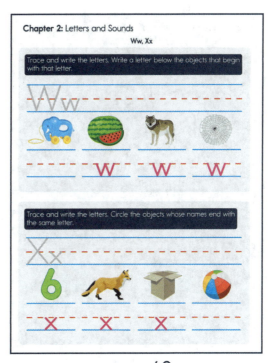

page 69

Answer Key

page 70

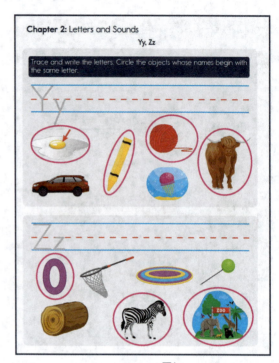

page 71

page 72

page 73

Answer Key

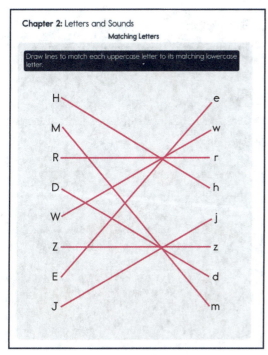

page 74

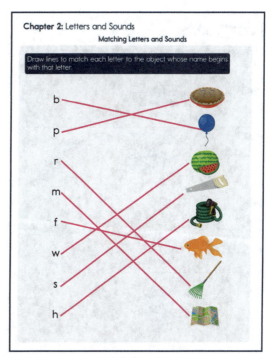

page 75

page 78

page 79

Answer Key

page 80

page 81

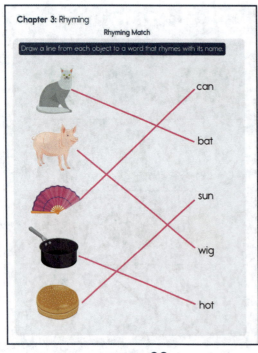

page 82

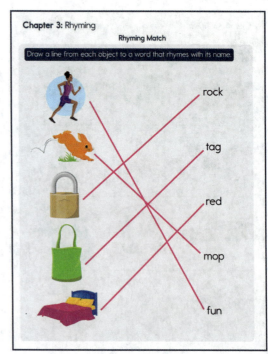

page 83

Answer Key

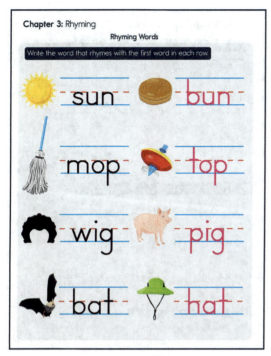

page 84

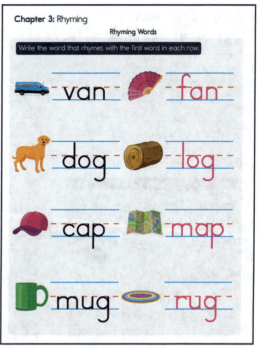

page 85

page 88

page 89

Answer Key

Chapter 4: High-Frequency Words

Read the words in the box. Trace the letters and then read each word.

and	to	me	big	little

and to me
big little

Read the sentences. Underline the words from the box.

The big dog can run to me.

The little dog can run to me.

The little dog can run and play here.

The big dog can run and play here.

page 90

Chapter 4: High-Frequency Words

Read the words in the box. Trace the letters and then read each word.

a	come	find	my	see

a come find
my see

Read the sentences. Underline the words from the box.

A boy and girl come to see my dog.

The boy and girl find my dog here.

My dog can come up to the boy and girl.

The boy and girl see my dog run and find the food.

page 91

Chapter 4: High-Frequency Words

Read the words in the box. Trace the letters and then read each word.

we	for	said	you	funny

we for said
you funny

Read the sentences. Underline the words from the box.

Mom said, "You can play ball."

Dad said, "You can play ball here."
The little boy said, "A ball for me!"

"We can play ball," said Dad.

The little boy is funny.

page 92

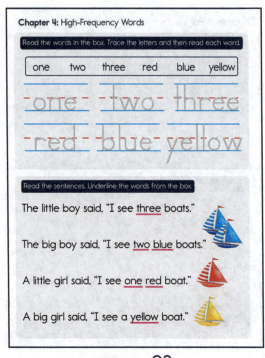

Chapter 4: High-Frequency Words

Read the words in the box. Trace the letters and then read each word.

one	two	three	red	blue	yellow

one two three
red blue yellow

Read the sentences. Underline the words from the box.

The little boy said, "I see three boats."

The big boy said, "I see two blue boats."

A little girl said, "I see one red boat."

A big girl said, "I see a yellow boat."

page 93

Spectrum Reading **Kindergarten**

Answer Key

page 94

page 95

page 99

Chapter 5: Fiction

Answer the questions.

1. What is Max doing?

   Max plays. Max rolls over.

2. How do you think Max feels?

   Max is happy.

3. What will Max do next?

   Max will shake off the grass.

4. Circle the sentence that matches the picture.

   Max rolls.
   Max hides.

page 101

Answer Key

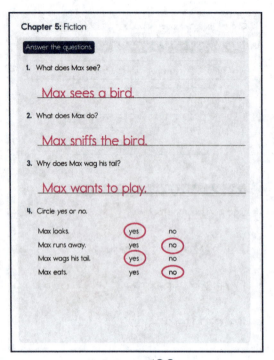

Chapter 5: Fiction

Answer the questions.

1. What does Max see?

   Max sees a bird.

2. What does Max do?

   Max sniffs the bird.

3. Why does Max wag his tail?

   Max wants to play.

4. Circle yes or no.

Max looks.	(yes)	no
Max runs away.	yes	(no)
Max wags his tail.	(yes)	no
Max eats.	yes	(no)

page 103

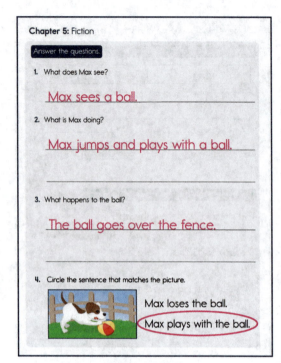

Chapter 5: Fiction

Answer the questions.

1. What does Max see?

   Max sees a ball.

2. What is Max doing?

   Max jumps and plays with a ball.

   _____

3. What happens to the ball?

   The ball goes over the fence.

   _____

4. Circle the sentence that matches the picture.

   Max loses the ball.

   (Max plays with the ball.)

page 105

Chapter 5: Fiction

Answer the questions.

1. What is Max looking into?

   Max looks in a mirror.

2. What does Max think he sees?

   Max thinks he sees another dog.

3. How does Max feel about what he sees?

   Max is happy.

4. Circle the sentence that matches the picture.

   Max sits.

   (Max wags his tail.)

page 107

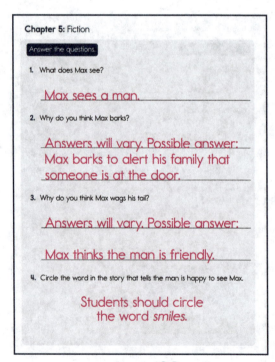

Chapter 5: Fiction

Answer the questions.

1. What does Max see?

   Max sees a man.

2. Why do you think Max barks?

   Answers will vary. Possible answer:
   Max barks to alert his family that
   someone is at the door.

3. Why do you think Max wags his tail?

   Answers will vary. Possible answer:

   Max thinks the man is friendly.

4. Circle the word in the story that tells the man is happy to see Max.

   Students should circle
   the word *smiles*.

page 109

Answer Key

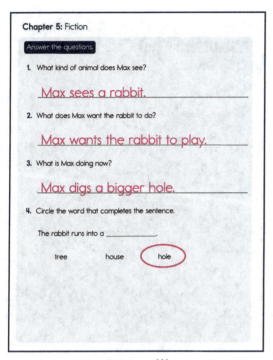

Chapter 5: Fiction

Answer the questions.

1. What kind of animal does Max see?

   Max sees a rabbit.

2. What does Max want the rabbit to do?

   Max wants the rabbit to play.

3. What is Max doing now?

   Max digs a bigger hole.

4. Circle the word that completes the sentence.

   The rabbit runs into a _____.

   tree   house   (hole)

page 111

Chapter 5: Fiction

Answer the questions.

1. What do you think Max is dreaming about?

   Max dreams about a bone.

2. Did Max's dream come true?

   Yes. A boy gives Max a bone.

Draw a picture of what you dream about.

Drawings will vary.

page 113

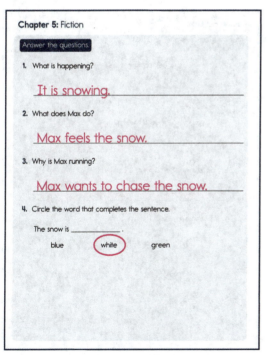

Chapter 5: Fiction

Answer the questions.

1. What is happening?

   It is snowing.

2. What does Max do?

   Max feels the snow.

3. Why is Max running?

   Max wants to chase the snow.

4. Circle the word that completes the sentence.

   The snow is _____.

   blue   (white)   green

page 115

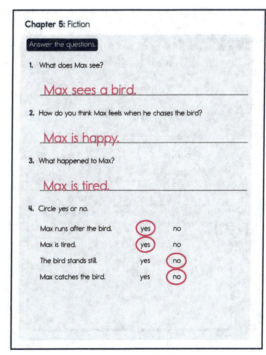

Chapter 5: Fiction

Answer the questions.

1. What does Max see?

   Max sees a bird.

2. How do you think Max feels when he chases the bird?

   Max is happy.

3. What happened to Max?

   Max is tired.

4. Circle yes or no.

   Max runs after the bird.   (yes)   no

   Max is tired.   (yes)   no

   The bird stands still.   yes   (no)

   Max catches the bird.   yes   (no)

page 117

Answer Key

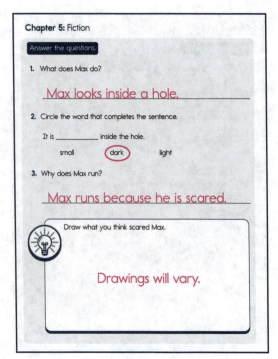

Chapter 5: Fiction

Answer the questions.

1. What does Max do?

   Max looks inside a hole.

2. Circle the word that completes the sentence.

   It is _____ inside the hole.

   small ~~(dark)~~ light

3. Why does Max run?

   Max runs because he is scared.

   Draw what you think scared Max.

   Drawings will vary.

page 119

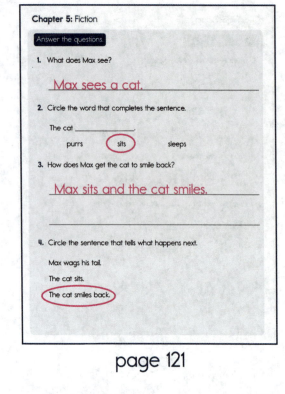

Chapter 5: Fiction

Answer the questions.

1. What does Max see?

   Max sees a cat.

2. Circle the word that completes the sentence.

   The cat _____.

   purrs ~~(sits)~~ sleeps

3. How does Max get the cat to smile back?

   Max sits and the cat smiles.

   _____

4. Circle the sentence that tells what happens next.

   Max wags his tail.

   The cat sits.

   ~~(The cat smiles back.)~~

page 121

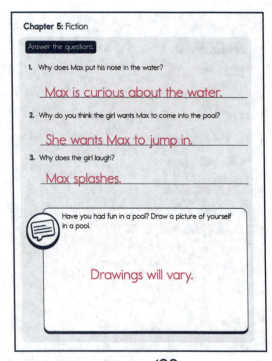

Chapter 5: Fiction

Answer the questions.

1. Why does Max put his nose in the water?

   Max is curious about the water.

2. Why do you think the girl wants Max to come into the pool?

   She wants Max to jump in.

3. Why does the girl laugh?

   Max splashes.

   Have you had fun in a pool? Draw a picture of yourself in a pool.

   Drawings will vary.

page 123

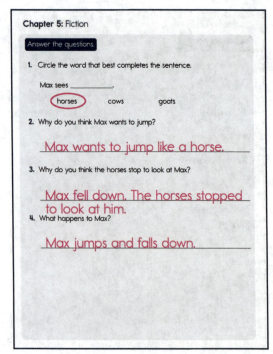

Chapter 5: Fiction

Answer the questions.

1. Circle the word that best completes the sentence.

   Max sees _____.

   ~~(horses)~~ cows goats

2. Why do you think Max wants to jump?

   Max wants to jump like a horse.

3. Why do you think the horses stop to look at Max?

   Max fell down. The horses stopped to look at him.

4. What happens to Max?

   Max jumps and falls down.

page 125

Answer Key

page 127

page 129

page 131

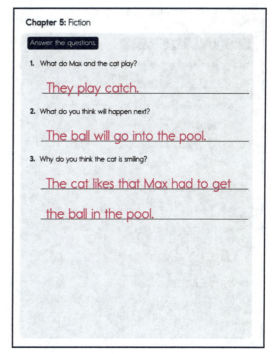

page 133

Answer Key

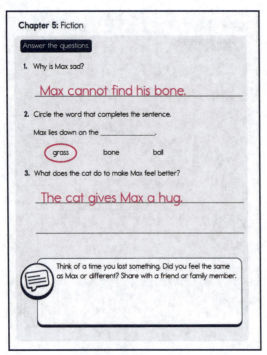

Chapter 5: Fiction

Answer the questions.

1. Why is Max sad?

   Max cannot find his bone.

2. Circle the word that completes the sentence.

   Max lies down on the _____.

   (grass)   bone   ball

3. What does the cat do to make Max feel better?

   The cat gives Max a hug.

   _____

Think of a time you lost something. Did you feel the same as Max or different? Share with a friend or family member.

page 135

Chapter 5: Fiction

Answer the questions.

1. Why does Max laugh when he looks in the mirror?

   He thinks he looks funny.

2. Where is the costume party?

   The party is at a friend's house.

3. What is funny about how Max and the cat are dressed?

   They dressed up as each other.

Draw a picture of yourself in a funny costume.

Drawings will vary.

page 137

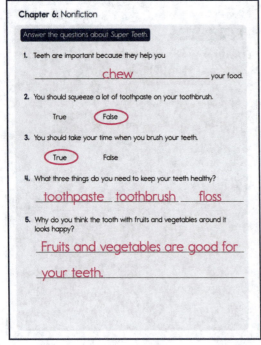

Chapter 6: Nonfiction

Answer the questions about *Super Teeth*.

1. Teeth are important because they help you

   _____ chew _____ your food.

2. You should squeeze a lot of toothpaste on your toothbrush.

   True   (False)

3. You should take your time when you brush your teeth.

   (True)   False

4. What three things do you need to keep your teeth healthy?

   toothpaste   toothbrush   floss

5. Why do you think the tooth with fruits and vegetables around it looks happy?

   Fruits and vegetables are good for

   your teeth.

page 141

Chapter 6: Nonfiction

Answer the questions.

1. It is easy to see animal tracks in the desert because it does not

   _____ rain _____ much there.

2. How many bobcat footprints do you count?

   _____ 11 _____

3. Which animal left a track that was not a footprint?

   gopher snake

4. There are no plants in the desert.   True   (False)

Where have you seen an animal track? What animal do you think it belonged to?

   Answers will vary.

   _____

page 143

Spectrum Reading **Kindergarten**

Answer Key

Chapter 6: Nonfiction

Answer the questions about *It All Makes Sense.*

1. What are your five senses?

   <u>sight</u>   <u>smell</u>

   <u>hearing</u>   <u>taste</u>

   <u>touch</u>

2. The bitter taste buds are found at the <u>back</u> of the tongue.

3. Ears tell your brain what they hear.

   (True)   False

   What is your favorite smell? Why?

   <u>Answers will vary.</u>

page 145

Chapter 6: Nonfiction

Answer the questions about *Apples.*

1. Where do apples grow?

   <u>Apples grow on trees.</u>

2. What kind of food is an apple?

   <u>Apples are a type of fruit.</u>

3. How can apples taste?

   <u>Apples can taste sweet or tart.</u>

   Do you like apples? Why or why not?

   <u>Answers will vary.</u>

page 147

Chapter 6: Nonfiction

Answer the questions about *Seals.*

1. Where are two places seals live?

   <u>water</u> and <u>on land</u>

2. What do seals have that make them good swimmers and divers?

   <u>Seals have flippers to make them</u>

   <u>good swimmers and divers.</u>

3. What keeps seals warm when the air is cold?

   <u>Seals have fur and a thick layer of</u>

   <u>fat to keep them warm.</u>

   What does the author say that seals do in water that surprises you? Write the sentence.

   <u>Answers will vary but could</u>
   include the sentence *They*
   even sleep in the water.

page 149

Chapter 6: Nonfiction

Answer the questions about *The First Cars.*

1. What did Henry Ford do?

   <u>Henry Ford made cars.</u>

2. Most people could buy these cars. Underline the sentence in the text that tells why. Students should underline the sentence *He built the first cars that were low enough in price for many people to buy them.*

3. What parts of a car cost extra money?

   <u>Bumpers and mirrors cost extra</u>

   <u>money.</u>

   The cars of the past were different from cars of today. Write one difference from the text.

   <u>Answers will vary.</u>

page 151

Answer Key

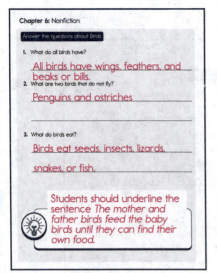

Chapter 6: Nonfiction

Answer the questions about *Birds*.

1. What do all birds have?
   All birds have wings, feathers, and beaks or bills.
2. What are two birds that do not fly?
   Penguins and ostriches

3. What do birds eat?
   Birds eat seeds, insects, lizards, snakes, or fish.

Students should underline the sentence *The mother and father birds feed the baby birds until they can find their own food.*

page 153

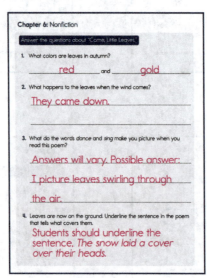

Chapter 6: Nonfiction

Answer the questions about *10 Reasons to Be a Farmer*.

1. Why would farmers get dirty?
   Answers will vary. Possible answer: Farmers work outside in the dirt.

2. What do you think *to harvest* means?
   to ride a tractor | (to pick the crops you grow)
   to feed animals | to save money

3. Farmers get to work with their community.
   (True) | False

What do you think the best reason to be a farmer is? Why?
   Answers will vary.

page 155

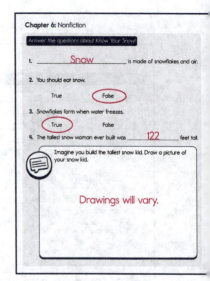

Chapter 6: Nonfiction

Answer the questions about *Know Your Snow!*

1. _____Snow_____ is made of snowflakes and air.

2. You should eat snow.
   True | (False)

3. Snowflakes form when water freezes.
   (True) | False

4. The tallest snow woman ever built was ___122___ feet tall.

Imagine you build the tallest snow kid. Draw a picture of your snow kid.
   Drawings will vary.

page 157

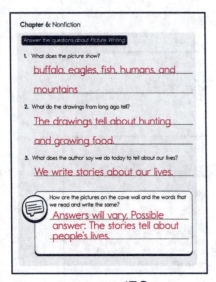

Chapter 6: Nonfiction

Answer the questions about *Picture Writing*.

1. What does the picture show?
   buffalo, eagles, fish, humans, and mountains
2. What do the drawings from long ago tell?
   The drawings tell about hunting and growing food.
3. What does the author say we do today to tell about our lives?
   We write stories about our lives.

How are the pictures on the cave wall and the words that we read and write the same?
   Answers will vary. Possible answer: The stories tell about people's lives.

page 159

Chapter 6: Nonfiction

Answer the questions about *"Come, Little Leaves."*

1. What colors are leaves in autumn?
   red and gold
2. What happens to the leaves when the wind comes?
   They came down.

3. What do the words *dance* and *sing* make you picture when you read this poem?
   Answers will vary. Possible answer: I picture leaves swirling through the air.
4. Leaves are now on the ground. Underline the sentence in the poem that tells what covers them.
   Students should underline the sentence, *The snow laid a cover over their heads.*

page 161

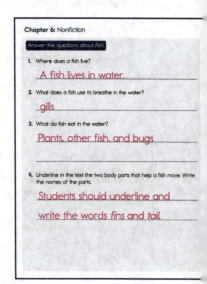

Chapter 6: Nonfiction

Answer the questions about *Fish*.

1. Where does a fish live?
   A fish lives in water.
2. What does a fish use to breathe in the water?
   gills
3. What do fish eat in the water?
   Plants, other fish, and bugs

4. Underline in the text the two body parts that help a fish move. Write the names of the parts.
   Students should underline and write the words *fins* and *tail.*

page 163

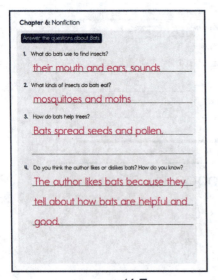

Chapter 6: Nonfiction

Answer the questions about *Bats*.

1. What do bats use to find insects?
   their mouth and ears, sounds
2. What kinds of insects do bats eat?
   mosquitoes and moths
3. How do bats help trees?
   Bats spread seeds and pollen.

4. Do you think the author likes or dislikes bats? How do you know?
   The author likes bats because they tell about how bats are helpful and good.

page 165

PHOTO CREDITS: page 146: ©BongrakArt/Shutterstock; page 148: ©Smit/Shutterstock; page 150: ©AH Creative Idea/Shutterstock; page 152: ©Randall Vermillion/Shutterstock; page 160: ©LilKar/Shutterstock; page 162: ©Fadhila Hasnah AW/Shutterstock; page 164: ©Passakorn Umpornmaha/Shutterstock